FAMILY PROMISES

KENNETH & GLORIA COPELAND

KENNETH COPELAND
PUBLICATIONS

Family Promises

ISBN-10 1-57562-118-5   30-0705
ISBN-13 978-1-57562-118-0

23 22 21 20 19 18   16 15 14 13 12 11

© 1997 Kenneth and Gloria Copeland

Kenneth Copeland Publications
Fort Worth, TX 76192-0001

TABLE of CONTENTS

PREFACE

"And all things, whatsoever ye shall ask
in prayer, believing, ye shall receive"
(Matthew 21:22).

I'll never forget the day Gloria and I settled forever that our children were not going to hell, but were going to live for God. Sitting in the middle of our bed with Bibles and concordances and lists of scriptures all around us, we agreed together in prayer that our children and every member of our family would be saved and serve God. We stood on God's promise in Matthew 18:19 that "if two of you shall agree on earth as touching any thing that they shall ask, it shall be done for them of my Father which is in heaven." We settled forever that we were a family without tragedy.

Well, that was many years ago, but we have never once backed off our stand of faith. And today, not only are our children saved and serving God, but all three of them and their families are working with us in the ministry.

How did we do it? By learning what rights and promises are given to us in the Word of God. Every time the devil came to kill, steal and destroy our children and our family, we looked for the scriptures we could use to combat the forces of the evil one. We stood on the promises of God in faith, and the power of God's Word got the job done!

It will get the job done for you and for your family too, if you'll take God's promises to heart and act on them. That's why we've put together this book of *Family Promises*. We want to help you get the truth of God's Word concerning your family fixed and established in your heart, and help you keep the Word of God before you at all times.

Read *Family Promises* over and over. Meditate on God's promises for your family. Confess them aloud daily. Stand on them in faith and act on them. Get your family together around the Communion table and settle forever that no member of your family will perish. Then when the devil comes around to try to destroy your marriage or steal your children, you can resist him with the Word—"As for me and my house, we will serve the Lord" (Joshua 24:15).

Kenneth and Gloria Copeland

Chapter 1

Blessings for Your Household

He blesses the dwelling
of the righteous.
Proverbs 3:33 (NASB)

Deuteronomy 4:40

NKJV—You shall therefore keep His statutes and His commandments which I command you today, that it may go well with you and with your children after you, and that you may prolong your days in the land which the Lord your God is giving you for all time.

NIV—Keep his decrees and commands, which I am giving you today, so that it may go well with you and your children after you and that you may live long in the land the Lord your God gives you for all time.

AMPC—Therefore you shall keep His statutes and His commandments, which I command you this day, that it may go well with you and your children after you, and that you may prolong your days in the land which the Lord your God gives you for ever.

Deuteronomy 11:18-21

KJV—Therefore shall ye lay up these my words in your heart and in your soul, and bind them for a sign upon your hand, that they may be as frontlets between your eyes. And ye shall teach them your children, speaking of them when thou sittest in thine house, and when thou walkest by the way, when thou liest down, and when thou risest up.

And thou shalt write them upon the door posts of thine house, and upon thy gates: That your days may be multiplied, and the days of your children, in the land which the Lord sware unto your fathers to give them, as the days of heaven upon the earth.

NIV—Fix these words of mine in your hearts and minds; tie them as symbols on your hands and bind them on your foreheads. Teach them to your children, talking about them when you sit at home and when you walk along the road, when you lie down and when you get up.

Write them on the doorframes of your houses and on your gates, so that your days and the days of your children may be many in the land that the Lord swore to give your forefathers, as many as the days that the heavens are above the earth.

NASB—You shall therefore impress these words of mine on your heart and on your soul; and you shall bind them as a sign on your hand, and they shall be as frontals on your forehead. And you shall teach them to your sons, talking of them when you sit in your house and when you walk along the road and when you lie down and when you rise up.

And you shall write them on the doorposts of your house and on your gates, so that your days and the days of your sons may be multiplied on the land which the Lord swore to your fathers to give them, as long as the heavens remain above the earth.

Deuteronomy 26:11

KJV—And thou shalt rejoice in every good thing which the Lord thy God hath given unto thee, and unto thine house.

AMPC—And you shall rejoice in all the good which the Lord your God has given you and your household.

Deuteronomy 28:8

KJV—The Lord shall command the blessing upon thee in thy storehouses, and in all that thou settest thine hand unto; and he shall bless thee in the land which the Lord thy God giveth thee.

NIV—The Lord will send a blessing on your barns and on everything you put your hand to. The Lord your God will bless you in the land he is giving you.

Joshua 1:7-8

KJV—Only be thou strong and very courageous, that thou mayest observe to do according to all the law, which Moses my servant commanded thee: turn not from it to the right hand or to the left, that thou mayest prosper whithersoever thou goest. This book of the law shall not depart out of thy mouth; but thou shalt meditate therein day and night, that thou mayest observe to do according to all that is written therein: for then thou shalt make thy way prosperous, and then thou shalt have good success.

NIV—Be strong and very courageous. Be careful to obey all the law my servant Moses gave you; do not turn from it to the right or to the left, that you may be successful wherever you go. Do not let this Book of the Law depart from your mouth; meditate on it day and night, so that you may be careful to do everything written in it. Then you will be prosperous and successful.

AMPC—Only you be strong, and very courageous, that you may do according to all the law, which Moses My servant commanded you. Turn not from it to the right hand or to the left, that you may prosper wherever you go. This book of the law shall not depart out of your mouth, but you shall meditate on it day and night, that you may observe and do according to all that is written in it; for then you shall make your way prosperous, and then you shall deal wisely and have good success.

Joshua 24:15

KJV—But as for me and my house, we will serve the Lord.

NIV—But as for me and my household, we will serve the Lord.

Psalm 4:8

NIV—For you alone, O Lord, make me dwell in safety.

AMPC—For You, Lord, alone make me dwell in safety and confident trust.

Psalm 91:10

KJV—There shall no evil befall thee, neither shall any plague come nigh thy dwelling.

NIV—Then no harm will befall you, no disaster will come near your tent.

AMPC—There shall no evil befall you, nor any plague or calamity come near your tent.

Psalm 101:2

KJV—I will walk within my house with a perfect heart.

AMPC—I will walk within my house in my integrity and with a blameless heart.

Psalm 112:1-3

NKJV—Blessed is the man who fears the Lord, who delights greatly in His commandments. His descendants will be mighty on earth; the generation of the upright will be blessed. Wealth and riches will be in his house, and his righteousness endures forever.

AMPC—Blessed—happy, fortunate [to be envied]—is the man who fears (reveres and worships) the Lord, who delights greatly in His commandments. His [spiritual] offspring shall be a mighty one upon earth; the generation of the upright shall be blessed. Prosperity and welfare are in his house, and his righteousness endures for ever.

Psalm 115:13-14

KJV—He will bless them that fear the Lord, both small and great. The Lord shall increase you more and more, you and your children.

AMPC—He will bless those who reverently and worshipfully fear the Lord, both small and great. The Lord give you increase more and more, you and your children.

Psalm 122:7

KJV—Peace be within thy walls, and prosperity within thy palaces.

NIV—May there be peace within your walls and security within your citadels.

Proverbs 1:33

KJV—But whoso hearkeneth unto me shall dwell safely, and shall be quiet from fear of evil.

NKJV—But whoever listens to me will dwell safely, and will be secure, without fear of evil.

NIV—But whoever listens to me will live in safety and be at ease, without fear of harm.

Proverbs 3:33

NKJV—[The Lord] blesses the habitation of the just.

NIV—[The Lord] blesses the home of the righteous.

AMPC—The curse of the Lord is in and on the house of the wicked, but He declares blessed—joyful and favored with blessings—the home of the just and consistently righteous.

Proverbs 12:7

KJV—The wicked are overthrown, and are not: but the house of the righteous shall stand.

NIV—Wicked men are overthrown and are no more, but the house of the righteous stands firm.

AMPC—The wicked are overthrown and are not, but the house of the [uncompromisingly] righteous shall stand.

Proverbs 13:22

KJV—A good man leaveth an inheritance to his children's children: and the wealth of the sinner is laid up for the just.

NIV—A good man leaves an inheritance for his children's children, but a sinner's wealth is stored up for the righteous.

AMPC—A good man leaves an inheritance [of moral stability and goodness] to his children's children, and the wealth of the sinner [finds its way eventually] into the hands of the righteous, for whom it was laid up.

Proverbs 14:11

KJV—The house of the wicked shall be overthrown: but the tabernacle of the upright shall flourish.

NKJV—The house of the wicked will be overthrown, but the tent of the upright will flourish.

NIV—The house of the wicked will be destroyed, but the tent of the upright will flourish.

Proverbs 14:26

NKJV—In the fear of the Lord there is strong confidence, and His children will have a place of refuge.

NIV—He who fears the Lord has a secure fortress, and for his children it will be a refuge.

AMPC—In the reverent and worshipful fear of the Lord is strong confidence, and His children shall always have a place of refuge.

Proverbs 15:6

KJV—In the house of the righteous is much treasure: but in the revenues of the wicked is trouble.

NIV—The house of the righteous contains great treasure, but the income of the wicked brings them trouble.

AMPC—In the house of the [uncompromisingly] righteous is great [priceless] treasure, but with the income of the wicked is trouble and vexation.

Proverbs 17:6

KJV—Children's children are the crown of old men; and the glory of children are their fathers.

NASB—Grandchildren are the crown of old men, and the glory of sons is their fathers.

Proverbs 21:20

NIV—In the house of the wise are stores of choice food and oil.

NASB—There is precious treasure and oil in the dwelling of the wise.

Proverbs 24:3-4

KJV—Through wisdom is an house builded; and by understanding it is established: And by knowledge shall the chambers be filled with all precious and pleasant riches.

NIV—By wisdom a house is built, and through understanding it is established; through knowledge its rooms are filled with rare and beautiful treasures.

AMPC—Through skillful and godly Wisdom is a house

[a life, a home, a family] built, and by understanding it is established [on a sound and good foundation]. And by knowledge shall the chambers [of its every area] be filled with all precious and pleasant riches.

Isaiah 54:13

KJV—And all thy children shall be taught of the Lord; and great shall be the peace of thy children.

AMPC—And all your [spiritual] children shall be disciples—taught of the Lord [and obedient to His will]; and great shall be the peace and undisturbed composure of your children.

NASB—And all your sons will be taught of the Lord; and the well-being of your sons will be great.

Isaiah 59:21

KJV—As for me, this is my covenant with them, saith the Lord; my spirit that is upon thee, and my words which I have put in thy mouth, shall not depart out of thy mouth, nor out of the mouth of thy seed, nor out of the mouth of thy seed's seed, saith the Lord, from henceforth and for ever.

NIV—"As for me, this is my covenant with them," says the Lord. "My Spirit, who is on you, and my words that I have put in your mouth will not depart from your mouth, or from the mouths of your children, or from the mouths of their descendants from this time on and forever," says the Lord.

AMPC—As for Me, this is My covenant or league with them, says the Lord: My Spirit Who is upon you [and Who writes the law of God inwardly in the heart], and

My words which I have put in your mouth, shall not depart out of your mouth, or out of the mouth of your [true, spiritual] children, or out of the mouth of your children's children, says the Lord, from henceforth and for ever.

Acts 2:39

KJV—For the promise is unto you, and to your children, and to all that are afar off, even as many as the Lord our God shall call.

AMPC—For the promise (of the Holy Spirit) is to and for you and your children, and to and for all that are far away, [even] to as many as the Lord our God invites and bids come to Himself.

Acts 16:31

KJV—Believe on the Lord Jesus Christ, and thou shalt be saved, and thy house.

NIV—Believe in the Lord Jesus, and you will be saved—you and your household.

AMPC—Believe in and on the Lord Jesus Christ—that is, give yourself up to Him, take yourself out of your own keeping and entrust yourself into His keeping, and you will be saved; [and this applies both to] you and your household as well.

Ephesians 4:26-27

NIV—"In your anger do not sin": Do not let the sun go down while you are still angry, and do not give the devil a foothold.

AMPC—When angry, do not sin; do not ever let your wrath—your exasperation, your fury or indignation—last until the sun goes down. Leave no [such] room or foothold for the devil—give no opportunity to him.

Weymouth—If angry, beware of sinning. Let not your irritation last until the sun goes down; and do not leave room for the devil.

Chapter
2

The Gift of Marriage

Walk in love, just as
Christ also loved you....
Ephesians 5:2 (NASB)

Proverbs 5:15

KJV—Drink waters out of thine own cistern, and running waters out of thine own well.

NIV—Drink water from your own cistern, running water from your own well.

AMPC—Drink waters out of your own cistern [of pure marriage relationship], and fresh running waters out of your own well.

Song of Solomon 7:10

KJV—I am my beloved's, and his desire is toward me.

NIV—I belong to my lover, and his desire is for me.

AMPC—[She proudly said] I am my beloved's, and his desire is toward me!

Song of Solomon 8:7

KJV—Many waters cannot quench love, neither can the floods drown it.

NIV—Many waters cannot quench love; rivers cannot wash it away.

NASB—Many waters cannot quench love, nor will rivers overflow it.

Mark 10:9

NKJV—Therefore what God has joined together, let not man separate.

AMPC—What therefore God has united—joined together—let not man separate or divide.

1 Corinthians 7:14

NIV—The unbelieving husband has been sanctified through his wife, and the unbelieving wife has been sanctified through her believing husband.

AMPC—The unbelieving husband is set apart (separated, withdrawn from heathen contamination and affiliated with the Christian people) by union with his consecrated (set-apart) wife; and the unbelieving wife is set apart and separated through union with her consecrated husband.

Weymouth—A woman who has an unbelieving husband—if he consents to live with her, let her not put him away. For the unbelieving husband is hallowed by union with a Christian woman, and the unbelieving wife is hallowed by union with a Christian brother.

1 Corinthians 11:3

KJV—But I would have you know, that the head of every man is Christ; and the head of the woman is the man; and the head of Christ is God.

AMPC—But I want you to know and realize that Christ is the head of every man, the head of a woman is her husband, and the Head of Christ is God.

1 Corinthians 13:4-8

NKJV—Love suffers long and is kind; love does not envy; love does not parade itself, is not puffed up; does not behave rudely, does not seek its own, is not provoked, thinks no evil; does not rejoice in iniquity, but rejoices in the truth; bears all things, believes all things, hopes all things, endures all things. Love never fails.

NIV—Love is patient, love is kind. It does not envy, it does not boast, it is not proud. It is not rude, it is not self-seeking, it is not easily angered, it keeps no record of wrongs. Love does not delight in evil but rejoices with the truth. It always protects, always trusts, always hopes, always perseveres. Love never fails.

AMPC—Love endures long and is patient and kind; love never is envious nor boils over with jealousy; is not boastful or vainglorious, does not display itself haughtily. It is not conceited—arrogant and inflated with pride; it is not rude (unmannerly), and does not act unbecomingly. Love [God's love in us] does not insist on its own rights or its own way, for it is not self-seeking; it is not touchy or fretful or resentful; it takes no account of the evil done to it—pays no attention to a suffered wrong. It does not rejoice at injustice and unrighteousness, but rejoices when right and truth prevail.

Love bears up under anything and everything that comes, is ever ready to believe the best of every person, its hopes are fadeless under all circumstances and it endures everything [without weakening]. Love never fails—never fades out or becomes obsolete or comes to an end.

Weymouth—Love is forbearing and kind. Love knows no jealousy. Love does not brag; is not conceited. She is not unmannerly, nor selfish, nor irritable, nor mindful of wrongs. She does not rejoice in injustice, but joyfully sides with the truth. She can overlook faults. She is full of trust, full of hope, full of endurance. Love never fails.

Ephesians 4:32

KJV—And be ye kind one to another, tenderhearted, forgiving one another, even as God for Christ's sake hath forgiven you.

NIV—Be kind and compassionate to one another, forgiving each other, just as in Christ God forgave you.

AMPC—And become useful and helpful and kind to one another, tenderhearted (compassionate, understanding, loving-hearted), forgiving one another [readily and freely], as God in Christ forgave you.

Weymouth—On the contrary, learn to be kind to one another, tenderhearted, forgiving one another, just as God in Christ has also forgiven you.

Ephesians 5:1

KJV—Be ye therefore followers of God, as dear children.

AMPC—Therefore be imitators of God—copy Him and follow His example—as well-beloved children [imitate their father].

Ephesians 5:21

KJV—Submitting yourselves one to another in the fear of God.

NIV—Submit to one another out of reverence for Christ.

AMPC—Be subject to one another out of reverence for Christ, the Messiah, the Anointed One.

Philippians 1:9-11

NKJV—And this I pray, that your love may abound still more and more in knowledge and all discernment, that you may approve the things that are excellent, that you may be sincere and without offense till the day of Christ, being filled with the fruits of righteousness which are by Jesus Christ, to the glory and praise of God.

NIV—And this is my prayer: that your love may abound more and more in knowledge and depth of insight, so that you may be able to discern what is best and may be pure and blameless until the day of Christ, filled with the fruit of righteousness that comes through Jesus Christ—to the glory and praise of God.

AMPC—And this I pray, that your love may abound yet more and more and extend to its fullest development in knowledge and all keen insight—that is, that your love may [display itself in] greater depth of acquaintance and more comprehensive discernment; so that you may surely learn to sense what is vital, and approve and prize what is excellent and of real value—recognizing the highest and the best, and distinguishing the moral differences; and that you may be untainted and pure and unerring and blameless, that—with hearts sincere and certain and unsullied—you may [approach] the day of Christ, not stumbling nor causing others to stumble. May you abound in and be filled with the fruits of righteousness (of right standing with God and right doing) which come through Jesus Christ, the Anointed One, to the honor and praise of God—that His glory may be both manifested and recognized.

Weymouth—And it is my prayer that your love may be more and more accompanied by clear knowledge and keen perception for testing things that differ, so that you may be men of transparent character, and may be blameless, in preparation for the day of Christ, being filled with those fruits of righteousness which come through Jesus Christ—to the glory and praise of God.

Colossians 3:14-15

NKJV—But above all these things put on love, which is the bond of perfection. And let the peace of God rule in your hearts, to which also you were called in one body; and be thankful.

NIV—And over all these virtues put on love, which binds them all together in perfect unity. Let the peace of Christ rule in your hearts, since as members of one body you were called to peace. And be thankful.

AMPC—And above all these [put on] love and enfold yourselves with the bond of perfectness—which binds everything together completely in ideal harmony. And let the peace (soul harmony which comes) from the Christ rule (act as umpire continually) in your hearts—deciding and settling with finality all questions that arise in your minds—[in that peaceful state] to which [as members of Christ's] one body you were also called [to live]. And be thankful—appreciative, giving praise to God always.

Weymouth—And over all these put on love, which is the perfect bond of union; and let the peace which Christ gives settle all questionings in your hearts, to which peace indeed you were called as belonging to His one body; and be thankful.

Hebrews 13:4

KJV—Marriage is honourable in all, and the bed undefiled.

NIV—Marriage should be honored by all, and the marriage bed kept pure.

AMPC—Let marriage be held in honor—esteemed worthy, precious, [that is,] of great price and especially dear—in all things. And thus let the marriage bed be (kept undishonored,) undefiled.

Weymouth—Let marriage be held in honor among all, and let the marriage bed be unpolluted.

1 Peter 3:8-9

NKJV—Finally, all of you be of one mind, having compassion for one another; love as brothers, be tenderhearted, be courteous; not returning evil for evil or reviling for reviling, but on the contrary blessing, knowing that you were called to this, that you may inherit a blessing.

AMPC—Finally, all [of you] should be of one and the same mind (united in spirit), sympathizing [with one another], loving [each the others] as brethren (of one household), compassionate and courteous—

tenderhearted and humble-minded. Never return evil for evil or insult for insult—scolding, tongue-lashing, berating; but on the contrary blessing—praying for their welfare, happiness and protection, and truly pitying and loving them. For know that to this you have been called, that you may yourselves inherit a blessing [from God]—obtain a blessing as heirs, bringing welfare and happiness and protection.

Weymouth—In conclusion, all of you should be harmonious, sympathetic, kind to the brethren, tender-hearted, lowly-minded, not requiting evil with evil nor abuse with abuse, but, on the contrary, giving a blessing, because a blessing is what you have been called by God to inherit.

Regarding Divorce

Malachi 2:16

KJV—For the Lord, the God of Israel, saith that he hateth putting away.

NIV—"I hate divorce," says the Lord God of Israel.

AMPC—For the Lord, the God of Israel, says: I hate divorce and marital separation.

Matthew 19:3-6

NKJV—The Pharisees also came to Him, testing Him, and saying to Him, "Is it lawful for a man to divorce his wife for just any reason?" And He answered and said to them, "Have you not read that He who made them at the beginning 'made them male and female,' and said, 'For this reason a man shall leave his father and mother and be joined to his wife, and the two shall become one flesh'? So then, they are no longer two but one flesh. Therefore what God has joined together, let not man separate."

NIV—Some Pharisees came to him to test him. They asked, "Is it lawful for a man to divorce his wife for any and every reason?" "Haven't you read," he replied, "that at the beginning the Creator 'made them male and female,' and said, 'For this reason a man will leave his father and mother and be united to his wife, and the two will become one flesh'? So they are no longer two, but one. Therefore what God has joined together, let man not separate."

Weymouth—Then came some of the Pharisees to Him to put Him to the proof by the question, "Has a man a right to divorce his wife for any sort of reason?" "Have you not read," He replied, "that He who made them 'made them' from the beginning 'male and female,' and said, 'for this reason a man shall leave his father and mother and cling to his wife, and the two shall be one'? Thus they are no longer two, but one. What therefore God has joined together, let not man separate."

1 Corinthians 7:10-13, 15-16

KJV—And unto the married I command, yet not I, but the Lord, Let not the wife depart from her husband: But and if she depart, let her remain unmarried, or be reconciled to her husband: and let not the husband put away his wife. But to the rest speak I, not the Lord: If any brother hath a wife that believeth not, and she be pleased to dwell with him, let him not put her away. And the woman which hath an husband that believeth not, and if he be pleased to dwell with her, let her not leave him....

But if the unbelieving depart, let him depart. A brother or a sister is not under bondage in such cases: but God hath called us to peace. For what knowest thou, O wife, whether thou shalt save thy husband? or how knowest thou, O man, whether thou shalt save thy wife?

NIV—To the married I give this command (not I, but the Lord): A wife must not separate from her husband. But if she does, she must remain unmarried or else be reconciled to her husband. And a husband must not divorce his wife. To the rest I say this (I, not the Lord): If any brother has a wife who is not a believer and she is willing to live with him, he must not divorce her. And if a woman has a husband who is not a believer and he is willing to live with her, she must not divorce him....

But if the unbeliever leaves, let him do so. A believing man or woman is not bound in such circumstances; God has called us to live in peace. How do you know, wife, whether you will save your husband? Or, how do you know, husband, whether you will save your wife?

AMPC—But to the married [people] I give charge, not I but the Lord, that the wife is not to separate from her husband. But if she does [separate from and divorce him], let her remain single or else be reconciled to her husband. And [I charge] the husband [also] that he should not put away or divorce his wife. To the rest I declare, I, not the Lord [for Jesus did not discuss this], that if any brother has a wife who does not believe [on

The Gift of Marriage

Christ], and she consents to live with him, he should not leave or divorce her. And if any woman has an unbelieving husband, and he consents to live with her, she should not leave or divorce him....

But if the unbelieving partner [actually] leaves, let him do so; in such [cases the remaining] brother or sister is not morally bound. But God has called us to peace. For, wife, how can you be sure of converting and saving your husband? Husband, how can you be sure of converting and saving your wife?

Family
Promises

Chapter 3

Husbands and Fathers

*Husbands, love your
wives, as Christ loved
the church and gave
Himself up for her.*
Ephesians 5:25 (AMPC)

Husbands

Proverbs 5:18-19

KJV—Let thy fountain be blessed: and rejoice with the wife of thy youth. Let her be as the loving hind and pleasant roe; let her breasts satisfy thee at all times; and be thou ravished always with her love.

NIV—May your fountain be blessed, and may you rejoice in the wife of your youth. A loving doe, a graceful deer—may her breasts satisfy you always, may you ever be captivated by her love.

AMPC—Let your fountain—of human life—be blessed [with the rewards of fidelity], and rejoice with the wife of your youth. Let her be as the loving hind and pleasant doe [tender, gentle, attractive]; let her bosom satisfy you at all times; and always be transported with delight in her love.

Proverbs 16:7

KJV—When a man's ways please the Lord, he maketh even his enemies to be at peace with him.

NIV—When a man's ways are pleasing to the Lord, he makes even his enemies live at peace with him.

Proverbs 18:22

KJV—Whoso findeth a wife findeth a good thing, and obtaineth favour of the Lord.

NIV—He who finds a wife finds what is good and receives favor from the Lord.

AMPC—He who finds a [true] wife finds a good thing, and obtains favor of the Lord.

1 Corinthians 7:3

NKJV—Let the husband render to his wife the affection due her, and likewise also the wife to her husband.

AMPC—The husband should give to his wife her conjugal rights—goodwill, kindness and what is due her as his wife; and likewise the wife to her husband.

Ephesians 5:25-33

KJV—Husbands, love your wives, even as Christ also loved the church, and gave himself for it; that he might sanctify and cleanse it with the washing of water by the word, that he might present it to himself a glorious church, not having spot, or wrinkle, or any such thing; but that it should be holy and without blemish.

So ought men to love their wives as their own bodies. He that loveth his wife loveth himself. For no man ever yet hated his own flesh; but nourisheth and cherisheth it, even as the Lord the church: For we are members of his body, of his flesh, and of his bones.

For this cause shall a man leave his father and mother, and shall be joined unto his wife, and they two shall be one flesh. This is a great mystery: but I speak concerning Christ and the church. Nevertheless let every one of you in particular so love his wife even as himself; and the wife see that she reverence her husband.

NIV—Husbands, love your wives, just as Christ loved the church and gave himself up for her to make her

Husbands and Fathers

holy, cleansing her by the washing with water through the word, and to present her to himself as a radiant church, without stain or wrinkle or any other blemish, but holy and blameless.

In this same way, husbands ought to love their wives as their own bodies. He who loves his wife loves himself. After all, no one ever hated his own body, but he feeds and cares for it, just as Christ does the church—for we are members of his body.

"For this reason a man will leave his father and mother and be united to his wife, and the two will become one flesh." This is a profound mystery—but I am talking about Christ and the church. However, each one of you also must love his wife as he loves himself, and the wife must respect her husband.

AMPC—Husbands, love your wives, as Christ loved the church and gave Himself up for her, so that He might sanctify her, having cleansed her by the washing of water with the Word, that He might present the church to Himself in glorious splendor, without spot or wrinkle or any such things—that she might be holy and faultless.

Even so husbands should love their wives as [being in a sense] their own bodies. He who loves his own wife loves himself. For no man ever hated his own flesh, but nourishes and carefully protects and cherishes it, as Christ does the church, because we are members (parts) of His body.

For this reason a man shall leave his father and his mother and shall be joined to his wife, and the two shall become one flesh. This mystery is very great, but I speak concerning [the relation of] Christ and the church. However, let each man of you (without exception) love his wife as [being in a sense] his very own self; and let the wife see that she respects and reverences her husband—that she notices him, regards him, honors him, prefers him, venerates and esteems him; and that she defers to him, praises him, and loves and admires him exceedingly.

Weymouth—Married men, love your wives, as Christ also loved the church and gave Himself up to death for her, in order to make her holy, cleansing her with the baptismal water by the word, that He might present the church to Himself a glorious bride, without spot or wrinkle or any other defect—holy and unblemished.

So, too, married men ought to love their wives as much as they love themselves. He who loves his wife loves himself. For never yet has a man hated his own body. On the contrary, he feeds and cherishes it, just as Christ feeds and cherishes the church; because we are, as it were, parts of His Body.

"For this reason a man is to leave his father and his mother and cling to his wife, and the two shall be as one flesh." That is a great truth hitherto kept secret: I mean the truth concerning Christ and the church. Yet I insist that among you also, each man is to love his own wife as much as he loves himself, and let a married woman see to it that she treats her husband with respect.

Colossians 3:19

NKJV—Husbands, love your wives and do not be bitter toward them.

AMPC—Husbands, love your wives—be affectionate and sympathetic with them—and do not be harsh or bitter or resentful toward them.

Weymouth—Married men, be affectionate to your wives, and do not treat them harshly.

1 Timothy 2:8

NKJV—Therefore I desire that the men pray everywhere, lifting up holy hands, without wrath and doubting.

AMPC—I desire therefore that in every place men should pray, without anger or quarreling or resentment or doubt [in their minds], lifting up holy hands.

Weymouth—So, then, I would have the men in every place of worship pray, lifting to God holy hands without anger or strife.

1 Timothy 5:8

NKJV—But if anyone does not provide for his own, and especially for those of his household, he has denied the faith and is worse than an unbeliever.

AMPC—If any one fails to provide for his relatives, and especially for those of his own family, he has disowned the faith [by failing to accompany it with fruits], and is worse than an unbeliever [who performs his obligation in these matters].

Weymouth—If a man makes no provision for his own relations, and especially for his own household, he has disowned the faith and is behaving worse than an unbeliever.

1 Peter 3:7

KJV—Likewise, ye husbands, dwell with [your wives]

according to knowledge, giving honour unto the wife, as unto the weaker vessel, and as being heirs together of the grace of life; that your prayers be not hindered.

NIV—Husbands, in the same way be considerate as you live with your wives, and treat them with respect as the weaker partner and as heirs with you of the gracious gift of life, so that nothing will hinder your prayers.

AMPC—In the same way you married men should live considerately with [your wives], with an intelligent recognition [of the marriage relation], honoring the woman as [physically] the weaker, but [realizing that you] are joint heirs of the grace (God's unmerited favor) of life, in order that your prayers may not be hindered and cut off. [Otherwise you cannot pray effectively.]

Fathering

Psalm 112:2

KJV—His seed shall be mighty upon earth: the generation of the upright shall be blessed.

NIV—His children will be mighty in the land; the generation of the upright will be blessed.

AMPC—His [spiritual] offspring shall be a mighty one upon earth; the generation of the upright shall be blessed.

Psalm 127:3-5

KJV—Lo, children are an heritage of the Lord: and the fruit of the womb is his reward. As arrows are in the hand of a mighty man; so are children of the youth. Happy is the man that hath his quiver full of them.

NKJV—Behold, children are a heritage from the Lord, the fruit of the womb is a reward. Like arrows in the hand of a warrior, so are the children of one's youth. Happy is the man who has his quiver full of them.

NIV—Sons are a heritage from the Lord, children a reward from him. Like arrows in the hands of a warrior are sons born in one's youth. Blessed is the man whose quiver is full of them.

Psalm 128:1-4

KJV—Blessed is every one that feareth the Lord; that walketh in his ways. For thou shalt eat the labour of thine hands: happy shalt thou be, and it shall be well with thee. Thy wife shall be as a fruitful vine by the sides of thine house: thy children like olive plants round about thy table. Behold, that thus shall the man be blessed that feareth the Lord.

NKJV—Blessed is every one who fears the Lord, who walks in His ways. When you eat the labor of your hands, you shall be happy, and it shall be well with you. Your wife shall be like a fruitful vine in the very heart of your house, your children like olive plants all around your table. Behold, thus shall the man be blessed who fears the Lord.

NIV—Blessed are all who fear the Lord, who walk in his ways. You will eat the fruit of your labor; blessings and prosperity will be yours. Your wife will be like a fruitful vine within your house; your sons will be like olive shoots around your table. Thus is the man blessed who fears the Lord.

Proverbs 13:22

KJV—A good man leaveth an inheritance to his children's children.

AMPC—A good man leaves an inheritance [of moral stability and goodness] to his children's children.

Proverbs 19:14

KJV—House and riches are the inheritance of fathers: and a prudent wife is from the Lord.

AMPC—House and riches are the inheritance from fathers, but a wise, understanding and prudent wife is from the Lord.

Proverbs 20:7

KJV—The just man walketh in his integrity: his children are blessed after him.

NIV—The righteous man leads a blameless life; blessed are his children after him.

AMPC—The righteous man walks in his integrity; blessed—happy, fortunate [enviable]—are his children after him.

Isaiah 38:19

KJV—The father to the children shall make known thy truth.

NIV—Fathers tell their children about your faithfulness.

AMPC—The father shall make known to the children Your faithfulness and Your truth.

NASB—A father tells his sons about Thy faithfulness.

Ephesians 6:4

KJV—And, ye fathers, provoke not your children to wrath: but bring them up in the nurture and admonition of the Lord.

NIV—Fathers, do not exasperate your children; instead, bring them up in the training and instruction of the Lord.

Weymouth—And you, fathers, do not irritate your children, but bring them up tenderly in the instruction and admonition of the Lord.

Colossians 3:21

KJV—Fathers, provoke not your children to anger, lest they be discouraged.

NIV—Fathers, do not embitter your children, or they will become discouraged.

Weymouth—Fathers, do not fret and harass your children, or you may make them sullen and morose.

1 Timothy 3:4

NIV—He must manage his own family well and see that his children obey him with proper respect.

AMPC—He must rule his own household well, keeping his children under control, with true dignity, commanding their respect in every way and keeping them respectful.

Weymouth—[He] must be...one who manages his own household well, keeping his children under control with true dignity.

41

---

*Husbands
and Fathers*

Chapter 4

Wives and Mothers

*An excellent wife, who
can find? For her worth
is far above jewels.*
Proverbs 31:10 (NASB)

Wives

Proverbs 11:16

KJV—A gracious woman retaineth honour: and strong men retain riches.

NIV—A kindhearted woman gains respect, but ruthless men gain only wealth.

AMPC—A gracious and good woman wins honor [for her husband], and violent men win riches; [but a woman who hates righteousness is a throne of dishonor for him].

Proverbs 12:4

KJV—A virtuous woman is a crown to her husband: but she that maketh ashamed is as rottenness in his bones.

NKJV—An excellent wife is the crown of her husband, but she who causes shame is like rottenness in his bones.

NIV—A wife of noble character is her husband's crown, but a disgraceful wife is like decay in his bones.

AMPC—A virtuous and worthy wife—earnest and strong in character—is a crowning joy to her husband, but she who makes ashamed is as rottenness in his bones.

Proverbs 14:1

KJV—Every wise woman buildeth her house: but the foolish plucketh it down with her hands.

NIV—The wise woman builds her house, but with her own hands the foolish one tears hers down.

AMPC—Every wise woman builds her house, but the foolish one tears it down with her own hands.

1 Corinthians 7:3

NKJV—Let the husband render to his wife the affection due her, and likewise also the wife to her husband.

AMPC—The husband should give to his wife her conjugal rights—goodwill, kindness and what is due her as his wife; and likewise the wife to her husband.

Ephesians 5:22-24

KJV—Wives, submit yourselves unto your own husbands, as unto the Lord. For the husband is the head of the wife, even as Christ is the head of the church: and he is the saviour of the body. Therefore as the church is subject unto Christ, so let the wives be to their own husbands in every thing.

NIV—Wives, submit to your husbands as to the Lord. For the husband is the head of the wife as Christ is the head of the church, his body, of which he is the Savior. Now as the church submits to Christ, so also wives should submit to their husbands in everything.

Weymouth—Married women, submit to your own husbands as if to the Lord; because a husband is the head of his wife, as Christ also is the head of the church, Himself the savior of the Body. And just as the church submits to Christ, so also married women should be entirely submissive to their husbands.

Ephesians 5:33

KJV—The wife see that she reverence her husband.

NIV—The wife must respect her husband.

AMPC—Let the wife see that she respects and reverences her husband—that she notices him, regards him, honors him, prefers him, venerates and esteems him; and that she defers to him, praises him, and loves and admires him exceedingly.

Weymouth—Let a married woman see to it that she treats her husband with respect.

Colossians 3:18

KJV—Wives, submit yourselves unto your own husbands, as it is fit in the Lord.

NIV—Wives, submit to your husbands, as is fitting in the Lord.

AMPC—Wives, be subject to your husbands—subordinate and adapt yourselves to them—as is right and fitting and your proper duty in the Lord.

1 Peter 3:1-5

NKJV—Wives, likewise, be submissive to your own husbands, that even if some do not obey the word, they, without a word, may be won by the conduct of their wives, when they observe your chaste conduct accompanied by fear. Do not let your adornment be merely outward—arranging the hair, wearing gold, or putting on fine apparel—rather let it be the hidden person of the heart, with the incorruptible beauty of a gentle and quiet spirit, which is very precious in the sight of God. For in this manner, in former times, the holy women who trusted in God also adorned themselves, being submissive to their own husbands.

NIV—Wives, in the same way be submissive to your husbands so that, if any of them do not believe the word, they may be won over without words by the behavior of their wives, when they see the purity and reverence of your lives. Your beauty should not come from outward adornment, such as braided hair and the wearing of gold jewelry and fine clothes. Instead, it should be that of your inner self, the unfading beauty of a gentle and quiet spirit, which is of great worth in God's sight. For this is the way the holy women of the past who put their hope in God used to make themselves beautiful. They were submissive to their own husbands.

Weymouth—Married women, in the same way, be submissive to your husbands, so that even if some of them disbelieve the word, they may, without a word being spoken, be won over by the daily life of their wives, after seeing your daily lives so chaste and reverent. Yours ought not to be the outward adornment of plaiting the hair, putting on jewels of gold, or wearing various dresses, but an inward beauty of nature, the imperishable ornament of a gentle and peaceful spirit, which is indeed precious in the sight of God. For this is how of old the holy women who set their hopes upon God used to adorn themselves, being submissive to their husbands.

Mothering

Psalm 147:13

KJV—For he hath strengthened the bars of thy gates; he hath blessed thy children within thee.

AMPC—For He has strengthened and made hard the bars of your gates; and He has blessed your children within you.

Proverbs 31:10-31

KJV—Who can find a virtuous woman? for her price is far above rubies. The heart of her husband doth safely trust in her, so that he shall have no need of spoil. She will do him good and not evil all the days of her life. She seeketh wool, and flax, and worketh willingly with her hands. She is like the merchants' ships; she bringeth her food from afar. She riseth also while it is yet night, and giveth meat to her household, and a portion to her maidens. She considereth a field, and buyeth it: with the fruit of her hands she planteth a vineyard. She girdeth her loins with strength, and strengtheneth her arms. She perceiveth that her merchandise is good: her candle goeth not out by night. She layeth her hands to the spindle, and her hands hold the distaff. She stretcheth out her hand to the poor; yea, she reacheth forth her hands to the needy.

She is not afraid of the snow for her household: for all her household are clothed with scarlet. She maketh herself coverings of tapestry; her clothing is silk and purple. Her husband is known in the gates, when he sitteth among the elders of the land. She maketh fine linen, and selleth it; and delivereth girdles unto the merchant. Strength and honour are her clothing; and she shall rejoice in time to come. She openeth her mouth with wisdom; and in her tongue is the law of kindness. She looketh well to the ways of her household, and eateth not the bread of idleness.

Her children arise up, and call her blessed; her husband also, and he praiseth her. Many daughters have done virtuously, but thou excellest them all. Favour is deceitful, and beauty is vain: but a woman that feareth the Lord, she shall be praised. Give her of the fruit of her hands; and let her own works praise her in the gates.

NKJV—Who can find a virtuous wife? For her worth is far above rubies. The heart of her husband safely trusts her; so he will have no lack of gain. She does him good and not evil all the days of her life.

She seeks wool and flax, and willingly works with her hands. She is like the merchant ships, she brings her food from afar. She also rises while it is yet night, and provides food for her household, and a portion for her maidservants. She considers a field and buys it; from her profits she plants a vineyard. She girds herself with strength, and strengthens her arms. She perceives that her merchandise is good, and her lamp does not go out by night. She stretches out her hands to the distaff, and her hand holds the spindle. She extends her hand to the poor, yes, she reaches out her hands to the needy.

She is not afraid of snow for her household, for all her household is clothed with scarlet. She makes tapestry for herself; her clothing is fine linen and purple. Her husband is known in the gates, when he sits among the elders of the land. She makes linen garments and sells them, and supplies sashes for the merchants. Strength and honor are her clothing; she shall rejoice in time to come. She opens her mouth with wisdom, and on her tongue is the law of kindness. She watches over the ways of her household, and does not eat the bread of idleness.

Her children rise up and call her blessed; her husband also, and he praises her: "Many daughters have done well, but you excel them all." Charm is deceitful and beauty is passing, but a woman who fears the Lord, she shall be praised. Give her of the fruit of her hands, and let her own works praise her in the gates.

NIV—A wife of noble character who can find? She is worth far more than rubies. Her husband has full confidence in her and lacks nothing of value. She brings him good, not harm, all the days of her life.

She selects wool and flax and works with eager hands. She is like the merchant ships, bringing her food from afar. She gets up while it is still dark; she provides food for her family and portions for her servant girls. She considers a field and buys it; out of her earnings she plants a vineyard. She sets about her work vigorously; her arms are strong for her tasks. She sees that her trading is profitable, and her lamp does not go out at night. In her hand she holds the distaff and grasps the spindle with her fingers. She opens her arms to the poor and extends her hands to the needy.

When it snows, she has no fear for her household; for all of them are clothed in scarlet. She makes coverings for her bed; she is clothed in fine linen and purple. Her husband is respected at the city gate, where he takes his seat among the elders of the land. She makes linen garments and sells them, and supplies the merchants with sashes. She is clothed with strength and dignity; she can laugh at the days to come. She speaks with wisdom, and faithful instruction is on her tongue. She watches over the affairs of her household and does not eat the bread of idleness.

Her children arise and call her blessed; her husband also, and he praises her: "Many women do noble things, but you surpass them all." Charm is deceptive, and beauty is fleeting; but a woman who fears the Lord is to be praised. Give her the reward she has earned, and let her works bring her praise at the city gate.

Titus 2:3-5

KJV—The aged women likewise, that they be in behaviour as becometh holiness, not false accusers, not given to much wine, teachers of good things; that they may teach the young women to be sober, to love their husbands, to love their children, to be discreet, chaste, keepers at home, good, obedient to their own husbands, that the word of God be not blasphemed.

NIV—Likewise, teach the older women to be reverent in the way they live, not to be slanderers or addicted to much wine, but to teach what is good. Then they can train the younger women to love their husbands and children, to be self-controlled and pure, to be busy at home, to be kind, and to be subject to their husbands, so that no one will malign the word of God.

AMPC—Bid the older women similarly to be reverent and devout in their deportment, as becomes those engaged in sacred service, not slanderers or slaves to drink. They are to give good counsel and be teachers of what is right and noble, so that they will wisely train the young women to be sane and sober-minded—temperate, disciplined—and to love their husbands and their children; to be self-controlled, chaste, homemakers, good-natured (kindhearted), adapting and subordinating themselves to their husbands, that the word of God may not be exposed to reproach—blasphemed or discredited.

Conceiving Children

Genesis 18:14

KJV—Is any thing too hard for the Lord? At the time appointed I will return unto thee, according to the time of life, and Sarah shall have a son.

AMPC—Is anything too hard or too wonderful for the Lord? At the appointed time, when the season [for her delivery] comes around, I will return to you and Sarah shall have borne a son.

Exodus 23:26

NKJV—No one shall suffer miscarriage or be barren in your land; I will fulfill the number of your days.

NIV—None will miscarry or be barren in your land. I will give you a full life span.

AMPC—None shall lose her young by miscarriage or be barren in your land; I will fulfill the number of your days.

Deuteronomy 7:13-14

KJV—And he will love thee, and bless thee, and multiply thee: he will also bless the fruit of thy womb.... Thou shalt be blessed above all people: there shall not be male or female barren among you, or among your cattle.

NKJV—And He will love you and bless you and multiply you; He will also bless the fruit of your womb.... You shall be blessed above all peoples; there shall not be a male or female barren among you or among your livestock.

NIV—He will love you and bless you and increase your numbers. He will bless the fruit of your womb.... You will be blessed more than any other people; none of your men or women will be childless, nor any of your livestock without young.

Deuteronomy 28:11

KJV—And the Lord shall make thee plenteous in goods, in the fruit of thy body, and in the fruit of thy cattle, and in the fruit of thy ground, in the land which the Lord sware unto thy fathers to give thee.

NKJV—And the Lord will grant you plenty of goods, in the fruit of your body, in the increase of your livestock, and in the produce of your ground, in the land of which the Lord swore to your fathers to give you.

NIV—The Lord will grant you abundant prosperity— in the fruit of your womb, the young of your livestock and the crops of your ground—in the land he swore to your forefathers to give you.

1 Samuel 1:27-28

KJV—For this child I prayed; and the Lord hath given me my petition which I asked of him: Therefore also I have lent him to the Lord; as long as he liveth he shall be lent to the Lord.

NIV—I prayed for this child, and the Lord has granted me what I asked of him. So now I give him to the Lord. For his whole life he will be given over to the Lord.

NASB—For this boy I prayed, and the Lord has given me my petition which I asked of Him. So I have also dedicated him to the Lord; as long as he lives he is dedicated to the Lord.

Psalm 113:9

KJV—He maketh the barren woman to keep house, and to be a joyful mother of children.

NIV—He settles the barren woman in her home as a happy mother of children.

AMPC—He makes the barren woman to be a homemaker, and a joyful mother of...children.

Luke 1:36-37

KJV—And, behold, thy cousin Elisabeth, she hath also conceived a son in her old age: and this is the sixth month with her, who was called barren. For with God nothing shall be impossible.

NIV—Even Elizabeth your relative is going to have a child in her old age, and she who was said to be barren is in her sixth month. For nothing is impossible with God.

Weymouth—And see, your relative Elizabeth—she also has conceived a son in her old age; and this is the sixth month with her who was called barren. For no promise from God will be impossible of fulfillment.

Hebrews 11:11

KJV—Through faith also Sarah herself received strength to conceive seed, and was delivered of a child when she was past age, because she judged him faithful who had promised.

AMPC—Because of faith also Sarah herself received physical power to conceive a child, even when she was long past the age for it, because she considered [God] Who had given her the promise, reliable and trustworthy and true to His word.

Weymouth—Through faith even Sarah herself received strength to become a mother—although she was past the time of life for this—because she judged Him faithful who had given the promise.

Wives and Mothers

Chapter 5

Parenting God's Way

Behold, children are a heritage from the Lord.

Psalm 127:3 (NKJV)

Genesis 18:19

KJV—For I know him, that he will command his children and his household after him, and they shall keep the way of the Lord, to do justice and judgment; that the Lord may bring upon Abraham that which he hath spoken of him.

NKJV—For I have known him, in order that he may command his children and his household after him, that they keep the way of the Lord, to do righteousness and justice, that the Lord may bring to Abraham what He has spoken to him.

NIV—For I have chosen him, so that he will direct his children and his household after him to keep the way of the Lord by doing what is right and just, so that the Lord will bring about for Abraham what he has promised him.

Deuteronomy 4:9-10

KJV—Only take heed to thyself, and keep thy soul diligently, lest thou forget the things which thine eyes have seen, and lest they depart from thy heart all the days of thy life: but teach them thy sons, and thy sons' sons; specially the day that thou stoodest before the Lord thy God in Horeb, when the Lord said unto me, Gather me the people together, and I will make them hear my words, that they may learn to fear me all the days that they shall live upon the earth, and that they may teach their children.

NIV—Only be careful, and watch yourselves closely so that you do not forget the things your eyes have seen or let them slip from your heart as long as you live. Teach them to your children and to their children after them. Remember the day you stood before the Lord your God at Horeb, when he said to me, "Assemble the people before me to hear my words so that they may learn to revere me as long as they live in the land and may teach them to their children."

AMPC—Only take heed, and guard your life diligently, lest you forget the things which your eyes have seen, and lest they depart from your [mind and] heart all the days of your life; teach them to your children, and your children's children; especially how on the day that you stood before the Lord your God in Horeb, the Lord said to me, Gather the people together to Me, and I will make them hear My words, that they may learn (reverently) to fear Me all the days they live upon the earth, and that they may teach their children.

Deuteronomy 6:6-7

KJV—And these words, which I command thee this day, shall be in thine heart: And thou shalt teach them diligently unto thy children, and shalt talk of them when thou sittest in thine house, and when thou walkest by the way, and when thou liest down, and when thou risest up.

NKJV—And these words which I command you today shall be in your heart. You shall teach them diligently to your children, and shall talk of them when you sit in your house, when you walk by the way, when you lie down, and when you rise up.

NIV—These commandments that I give you today

are to be upon your hearts. Impress them on your children. Talk about them when you sit at home and when you walk along the road, when you lie down and when you get up.

Deuteronomy 11:18-21

KJV—Therefore shall ye lay up these my words in your heart and in your soul, and bind them for a sign upon your hand, that they may be as frontlets between your eyes. And ye shall teach them your children, speaking of them when thou sittest in thine house, and when thou walkest by the way, when thou liest down, and when thou risest up. And thou shalt write them upon the door posts of thine house, and upon thy gates: That your days may be multiplied, and the days of your children, in the land which the Lord sware unto your fathers to give them, as the days of heaven upon the earth.

NIV—Fix these words of mine in your hearts and minds; tie them as symbols on your hands and bind them on your foreheads. Teach them to your children, talking about them when you sit at home and when you walk along the road, when you lie down and when you get up. Write them on the doorframes of your houses and on your gates, so that your days and the days of your children may be many in the land that the Lord swore to give your forefathers, as many as the days that the heavens are above the earth.

Proverbs 13:24

KJV—He that spareth his rod hateth his son: but he that loveth him chasteneth him betimes [quickly].

NKJV—He who spares his rod hates his son, but he who loves him disciplines him promptly.

NIV—He who spares the rod hates his son, but he who loves him is careful to discipline him.

AMPC—He who spares his rod [of discipline] hates his son, but he who loves him diligently disciplines and punishes him early.

Proverbs 19:18

KJV—Chasten thy son while there is hope, and let not thy soul spare for his crying.

NKJV—Chasten your son while there is hope, and do not set your heart on his destruction.

NIV—Discipline your son, for in that there is hope; do not be a willing party to his death.

AMPC—Discipline your son while there is hope, but do not [indulge your angry resentments by undue chastisements and] set yourself to his ruin.

Proverbs 22:6

KJV—Train up a child in the way he should go: and when he is old, he will not depart from it.

NIV—Train a child in the way he should go, and when he is old he will not turn from it.

AMPC—Train up a child in the way he should go [and in keeping with his individual gift or bent], and when he is old he will not depart from it.

Proverbs 22:15

KJV—Foolishness is bound up in the heart of a child; the rod of correction will drive it far from him.

NIV—Folly is bound up in the heart of a child, but the rod of discipline will drive it far from him.

Proverbs 23:13-14

NIV—Do not withhold discipline from a child; if you punish him with the rod, he will not die. Punish him with the rod and save his soul from death.

Proverbs 23:24-25

KJV—The father of the righteous shall greatly rejoice: and he that begetteth a wise child shall have joy of him. Thy father and thy mother shall be glad, and she that bare thee shall rejoice.

NKJV—The father of the righteous will greatly rejoice, and he who begets a wise child will delight in him. Let your father and your mother be glad, and let her who bore you rejoice.

NIV—The father of a righteous man has great joy; he who has a wise son delights in him. May your father and mother be glad; may she who gave you birth rejoice!

Proverbs 29:15

KJV—The rod and reproof give wisdom.

NIV—The rod of correction imparts wisdom.

Proverbs 29:17

KJV—Correct thy son, and he shall give thee rest; yea, he shall give delight unto thy soul.

NIV—Discipline your son, and he will give you peace; he will bring delight to your soul.

NASB—Correct your son, and he will give you comfort; he will also delight your soul.

Isaiah 44:3

KJV—I will pour my spirit upon thy seed, and my blessing upon thine offspring.

NKJV—I will pour My Spirit on your descendants, and My blessing on your offspring.

NIV—I will pour out my Spirit on your offspring, and my blessing on your descendants.

Isaiah 54:13

KJV—And all thy children shall be taught of the Lord; and great shall be the peace of thy children.

AMPC—And all your [spiritual] children shall be disciples—taught of the Lord [and obedient to His will]; and great shall be the peace and undisturbed composure of your children.

NASB—And all your sons will be taught of the Lord; and the well-being of your sons will be great.

Malachi 4:6

KJV—And he shall turn the heart of the fathers to the children, and the heart of the children to their fathers, lest I come and smite the earth with a curse.

AMPC—And he shall turn [and reconcile] the hearts of the [estranged] fathers to the [ungodly] children, and the hearts of the [rebellious] children to [the piety of] their fathers [a reconciliation produced by repentance of the ungodly]; lest I come and smite the land with a curse [and a ban of utter destruction].

64

Family
Promises

Chapter 6

Promises for Children

*Let no one look down
on your youthfulness,
but rather in speech,
conduct, love, faith
and purity, show
yourself an example of
those who believe.*
1 Timothy 4:12 (NASB)

Proverbs 4:1

KJV—Hear, ye children, the instruction of a father, and attend to know understanding.

NKJV—Hear, my children, the instruction of a father, and give attention to know understanding.

NIV—Listen, my sons, to a father's instruction; pay attention and gain understanding.

Proverbs 6:20-22

KJV—My son, keep thy father's commandment, and forsake not the law of thy mother: Bind them continually upon thine heart, and tie them about thy neck. When thou goest, it shall lead thee; when thou sleepest, it shall keep thee; and when thou awakest, it shall talk with thee.

NIV—My son, keep your father's commands and do not forsake your mother's teaching. Bind them upon your heart forever; fasten them around your neck. When you walk, they will guide you; when you sleep, they will watch over you; when you awake, they will speak to you.

AMPC—My son, keep your father's [God-given] commandment, and forsake not the law of [God] your mother [taught you]. Bind them continually upon your heart, and tie them about your neck. When you go, [the Word of your parents' God] it shall lead you; when you sleep, it shall keep you, and when you waken, it shall talk with you.

Proverbs 13:1

KJV—A wise son heareth his father's instruction.

NKJV—A wise son heeds his father's instruction.

Proverbs 15:5

KJV—A fool despiseth his father's instruction: but he that regardeth reproof is prudent.

NKJV—A fool despises his father's instruction, but he who receives correction is prudent.

NIV—A fool spurns his father's discipline, but whoever heeds correction shows prudence.

Proverbs 20:11

KJV—Even a child is known by his doings, whether his work be pure, and whether it be right.

NIV—Even a child is known by his actions, by whether his conduct is pure and right.

AMPC—Even a child is known by his acts, whether or not what he does is pure and right.

Proverbs 23:22

KJV—Hearken unto thy father that begat thee, and despise not thy mother when she is old.

NKJV—Listen to your father who begot you, and do not despise your mother when she is old.

NIV—Listen to your father, who gave you life, and do not despise your mother when she is old.

Proverbs 28:7

KJV—Whoso keepeth the law is a wise son: but he that is a companion of riotous men shameth his father.

NKJV—Whoever keeps the law is a discerning son, but a companion of gluttons shames his father.

NIV—He who keeps the law is a discerning son, but a companion of gluttons disgraces his father.

AMPC—Whoever keeps the law [of God and man] is a wise son, but he who is a companion of gluttons and the carousing, self-indulgent and extravagant shames his father.

Matthew 18:10

KJV—Take heed that ye despise not one of these little ones; for I say unto you, that in heaven their angels do always behold the face of my Father which is in heaven.

NIV—See that you do not look down on one of these little ones. For I tell you that their angels in heaven always see the face of my Father in heaven.

AMPC—Beware that you do not despise or feel scornful toward or think little of one of these little ones, for I tell you that in heaven their angels always are in the presence of and look upon the face of My Father Who is in heaven.

Luke 2:40

NKJV—And the Child grew and became strong in spirit, filled with wisdom; and the grace of God was upon Him.

NIV—And the child grew and became strong; he was filled with wisdom, and the grace of God was upon him.

AMPC—And the Child grew and became strong in spirit, filled with wisdom, and the grace (favor and spiritual blessing) of God was upon Him.

Ephesians 6:1-3

KJV—Children, obey your parents in the Lord: for this is right. Honour thy father and mother; which is the first commandment with promise; that it may be well with thee, and thou mayest live long on the earth.

*Promises
for Children*

NIV—Children, obey your parents in the Lord, for this is right. "Honor your father and mother"—which is the first commandment with a promise—"that it may go well with you and that you may enjoy long life on the earth."

Weymouth—Children, be obedient to your parents as a Christian duty, for this is right. "Honor your father and your mother"—this is the first commandment which has a promise added to it—"so that it may be well with you, and that you may live long on the earth."

Colossians 3:20

KJV—Children, obey your parents in all things: for this is well pleasing unto the Lord.

NIV—Children, obey your parents in everything, for this pleases the Lord.

Weymouth—Children, be obedient to your parents in everything; for that is well-pleasing in the Lord.

1 Timothy 4:12

NKJV—Let no one despise your youth, but be an example to the believers in word, in conduct, in love, in spirit, in faith, in purity.

NIV—Don't let anyone look down on you because you are young, but set an example for the believers in speech, in life, in love, in faith and in purity.

AMPC—Let no one despise or think less of you because of your youth, but be an example (pattern) for the believers, in speech, in conduct, in love, in faith and in purity.

NASB—Let no one look down on your youthfulness, but rather in speech, conduct, love, faith and purity, show yourself an example of those who believe.

2 Timothy 2:22

KJV—Flee also youthful lusts: but follow righteousness, faith, charity, peace, with them that call on the Lord out of a pure heart.

NIV—Flee the evil desires of youth, and pursue righteousness, faith, love and peace, along with those who call on the Lord out of a pure heart.

Weymouth—Curb the cravings of youth; and strive

for integrity, faith, love, peace, in company with all who pray to the Lord with pure hearts.

Hebrews 12:9-11

NKJV—Furthermore, we have had human fathers who corrected us, and we paid them respect. Shall we not much more readily be in subjection to the Father of spirits and live? For they indeed for a few days chastened us as seemed best to them, but He for our profit, that we may be partakers of His holiness. Now no chastening seems to be joyful for the present, but painful; nevertheless, afterward it yields the peaceable fruit of righteousness to those who have been trained by it.

NIV—Moreover, we have all had human fathers who disciplined us and we respected them for it. How much more should we submit to the Father of our spirits and live! Our fathers disciplined us for a little while as they thought best; but God disciplines us for our good, that we may share in his holiness. No discipline seems pleasant at the time, but painful. Later on, however, it produces a harvest of righteousness and peace for those who have been trained by it.

AMPC—Moreover, we have had earthly fathers who disciplined us and we yielded [to them] and respected [them for training us]. Shall we not much more cheerfully submit to the Father of spirits and so [truly] live? For [our earthly fathers] disciplined us for only a short period of time and chastised us as seemed proper and good to them, but He disciplines us for our certain good, that we may become sharers in His own holiness. For the time being no discipline brings joy but seems grievous and painful, but afterwards it yields peaceable fruit of righteousness to those who have been trained by it—a harvest of fruit which consists in righteousness, [that is, in conformity to God's will in purpose, thought and action, resulting in right living and right standing with God].

Family
Promises

Chapter 7

Single—And Married to Him

*Your Maker is your
husband—the Lord
Almighty is his name—the
Holy One of Israel is your
Redeemer; he is called
the God of all the earth....
Isaiah 54:5 (NIV)*

Exodus 22:22-23

KJV—Ye shall not afflict any widow, or fatherless child. If thou afflict them in any wise, and they cry at all unto me, I will surely hear their cry.

NKJV—You shall not afflict any widow or fatherless child. If you afflict them in any way, and they cry at all to Me, I will surely hear their cry.

NIV—Do not take advantage of a widow or an orphan. If you do and they cry out to me, I will certainly hear their cry.

Deuteronomy 14:29

KJV—The fatherless, and the widow, which are within thy gates, shall come, and shall eat and be satisfied.

NKJV—The fatherless and the widow who are within your gates, may come and eat and be satisfied.

NIV—The fatherless and the widows who live in your towns may come and eat and be satisfied.

Psalm 68:5

KJV—A father of the fatherless, and a judge of the widows, is God in his holy habitation.

NIV—A father to the fatherless, a defender of widows, is God in his holy dwelling.

AMPC—A father of the fatherless, and a judge and protector of the widows, is God in His holy habitation.

Psalm 68:6

NIV—God sets the lonely in families.

AMPC—God places the solitary in families and gives the desolate a home in which to dwell.

NASB—God makes a home for the lonely.

Psalm 146:9

KJV—The Lord preserveth the strangers; he relieveth the fatherless and widow.

NKJV—The Lord watches over the strangers; He relieves the fatherless and widow.

NIV—The Lord watches over the alien and sustains the fatherless and the widow.

Proverbs 15:25

KJV—The Lord will destroy the house of the proud: but he will establish the border of the widow.

NKJV—The Lord will destroy the house of the proud, but He will establish the boundary of the widow.

NIV—The Lord tears down the proud man's house but he keeps the widow's boundaries intact.

Isaiah 54:5

KJV—For thy Maker is thine husband; the Lord of hosts is his name; and thy Redeemer the Holy One of Israel; The God of the whole earth shall he be called.

NKJV—For your Maker is your husband, the Lord of hosts is His name; and your Redeemer is the Holy One of Israel; He is called the God of the whole earth.

NIV—For your Maker is your husband—the Lord Almighty is his name—the Holy One of Israel is your Redeemer; he is called the God of all the earth.

Jeremiah 29:11

KJV—For I know the thoughts that I think toward you, saith the Lord, thoughts of peace, and not of evil, to give you an expected end.

AMPC—For I know the thoughts and plans that I have for you, says the Lord, thoughts and plans for welfare and peace, and not for evil, to give you hope in your final outcome.

NASB—"For I know the plans I have for you," declares the Lord, "plans to prosper you and not to harm you, plans to give you hope and a future."

Jeremiah 49:11

KJV—Leave thy fatherless children, I will preserve them alive; and let thy widows trust in me.

NIV—Leave your orphans; I will protect their lives. Your widows too can trust in me.

AMPC—Leave your fatherless children, I will [do what is necessary to] preserve them alive; and let [those made] your widows trust and confide in Me.

1 Corinthians 7:32

NKJV—But I want you to be without care. He who is unmarried cares for the things that belong to the Lord—how he may please the Lord.

NIV—I would like you to be free from concern. An unmarried man is concerned about the Lord's affairs—how he can please the Lord.

AMPC—My desire is to have you free from all anxiety and distressing care. The unmarried [man] is anxious about the things of the Lord, how he may please the Lord.

1 Corinthians 7:34

NKJV—There is a difference between a wife and a virgin. The unmarried woman cares about the things of the Lord, that she may be holy both in body and in spirit.

NIV—An unmarried woman or virgin is concerned about the Lord's affairs: Her aim is to be devoted to the Lord in both body and spirit.

AMPC—And the unmarried woman or girl is concerned and anxious about the matters of the Lord, how to be wholly separated and set apart in body and spirit.

1 Timothy 5:3-5

KJV—Honour widows that are widows indeed.... Now she that is a widow indeed, and desolate, trusteth in God, and continueth in supplications and prayers night and day.

NIV—Give proper recognition to those widows who are really in need.... The widow who is really in need and left all alone puts her hope in God and continues night and day to pray and to ask God for help.

AMPC—[Always] treat with great consideration and give aid to those who are truly widowed—solitary and without support.... Now [a woman] who is a real widow, and is left entirely alone and desolate, has fixed her hope on God and perseveres in supplications and prayers night and day.

James 1:27

KJV—Pure religion and undefiled before God and the Father is this, to visit the fatherless and widows in their affliction, and to keep himself unspotted from the world.

NIV—Religion that God our Father accepts as pure and faultless is this: to look after orphans and widows in their distress and to keep oneself from being polluted by the world.

Weymouth—The religion which is pure and stainless in the sight of our God and Father is to visit orphans and widows in their time of trouble, and to keep one's own self unspotted from the world.

Chapter 8

Brothers and Sisters in the Lord

*Now therefore ye
are no more strangers
and foreigners, but
fellowcitizens with
the saints, and of the
household of God.
Ephesians 2:19* (KJV)

Psalm 133:1

KJV—Behold, how good and how pleasant it is for brethren to dwell together in unity!

NIV—How good and pleasant it is when brothers live together in unity!

NASB—Behold, how good and how pleasant it is for brothers to dwell together in unity!

Proverbs 17:17

KJV—A friend loveth at all times, and a brother is born for adversity.

NIV—A friend loves at all times, and a brother is born for adversity.

AMPC—A friend loves at all times, and is born, as is a brother, for adversity.

Ecclesiastes 4:9-12

KJV—Two are better than one; because they have a good reward for their labour. For if they fall, the one will lift up his fellow: but woe to him that is alone when he falleth; for he hath not another to help him up. Again, if two lie together, then they have heat: but how can one be warm alone? And if one prevail against him, two shall withstand him; and a threefold cord is not quickly broken.

NKJV—Two are better than one, because they have a good reward for their labor. For if they fall, one will lift up his companion. But woe to him who is alone when he falls, for he has no one to help him up. Again, if two lie down together, they will keep warm; but how can one be warm alone? Though one may be overpowered by another, two can withstand him. And a threefold cord is not quickly broken.

AMPC—Two are better than one, because they have a good [more satisfying] reward for their labor; for if they fall, the one will lift up his fellow. But woe to him who is alone when he falls and has not another to lift him up! Again, if two lie together, then they have warmth; but how can one be warm alone? And though a man might prevail against him who is alone, two will withstand him. A threefold cord is not quickly broken.

Matthew 6:14

KJV—For if ye forgive men their trespasses, your heavenly Father will also forgive you.

Brothers and Sister in the Lord

NIV—For if you forgive men when they sin against you, your heavenly Father will also forgive you.

AMPC—For if you forgive people their trespasses— that is, their reckless and willful sins, leaving them, letting them go and giving up resentment—your heavenly Father will also forgive you.

Matthew 18:18-20

KJV—Verily I say unto you, Whatsoever ye shall bind on earth shall be bound in heaven: and whatsoever ye shall loose on earth shall be loosed in heaven. Again I say unto you, that if two of you shall agree on earth as touching any thing that they shall ask, it shall be done for them of my Father which is in heaven. For where two or three are gathered together in my name, there am I in the midst of them.

NIV—I tell you the truth, whatever you bind on earth will be bound in heaven, and whatever you loose on earth will be loosed in heaven. Again, I tell you that if two of you on earth agree about anything you ask for, it will be done for you by my Father in heaven. For where two or three come together in my name, there am I with them.

Matthew 22:39

NKJV—You shall love your neighbor as yourself.

AMPC—You shall love your neighbor as [you do] yourself.

Matthew 25:35-40

NKJV—'For I was hungry and you gave Me food; I was thirsty and you gave Me drink; I was a stranger and you took Me in; I was naked and you clothed Me; I was sick and you visited Me; I was in prison and you came to Me.' "Then the righteous will answer Him, saying, 'Lord, when did we see You hungry and feed You, or thirsty and give You drink? When did we see You a stranger and take You in, or naked and clothe You? Or when did we see You sick, or in prison, and come to You?' And the King will answer and say to them, 'Assuredly, I say to you, inasmuch as you did it to one of the least of these My brethren, you did it to Me.'"

NIV—'For I was hungry and you gave me something to eat, I was thirsty and you gave me something to drink, I was a stranger and you invited me in, I needed clothes and you clothed me, I was sick and you looked after me, I was in prison and you came to visit me.' "Then the righteous will answer him, 'Lord, when did we see you hungry and feed you, or thirsty and give you something to drink? When did we see you a stranger and invite you in, or needing clothes and clothe you? When did we see you sick or in prison and go to visit you?' "The King will reply, 'I tell you the truth, whatever you did for one of the least of these brothers of mine, you did for me.'"

AMPC—For I was hungry and you gave Me food; I was thirsty and you gave Me something to drink; I was a stranger and you brought Me together with yourselves and welcomed and entertained and lodged Me; I was naked and you clothed Me; I was sick and you visited Me with help and ministering care; I was in prison and you came to see Me. Then the just and upright will answer Him, Lord, when did we see You hungry and gave You food, or thirsty and gave You something to drink? And when did we see You a stranger and welcomed and entertained You, or naked and clothed You? And when did we see You sick or in prison and came to visit You? And the King will reply to them, truly, I tell you, in as far as you did it to one of the least [in the estimation of men] of these My brethren, you did it to Me.

John 13:34

KJV—A new commandment I give unto you, that ye love one another; as I have loved you, that ye also love one another.

NIV—A new command I give you: Love one another. As I have loved you, so you must love one another.

Weymouth—A new commandment I give you, to love one another; that as I have loved you, you also may love one another.

John 15:12

KJV—This is my commandment, that ye love one another, as I have loved you.

NIV—My command is this: Love each other as I have loved you.

AMPC—This is My commandment, that you love one another [just] as I have loved you.

Romans 12:10

KJV—Be kindly affectioned one to another with brotherly love; in honour preferring one another.

NIV—Be devoted to one another in brotherly love. Honor one another above yourselves.

AMPC—Love one another with brotherly affection— as members of one family—giving precedence and showing honor to one another.

Galatians 3:26

KJV—For ye are all the children of God by faith in Christ Jesus.

NIV—You are all sons of God through faith in Christ Jesus.

AMPC—For in Christ Jesus you are all sons of God through faith.

Galatians 3:28-29

KJV—There is neither Jew nor Greek, there is neither bond nor free, there is neither male nor female: for ye are all one in Christ Jesus. And if ye be Christ's, then are ye Abraham's seed, and heirs according to the promise.

AMPC—There is [now no distinction], neither Jew nor Greek, there is neither slave nor free, there is not male and female; for you are all one in Christ Jesus. And if you belong to Christ (are in Him, Who is Abraham's Seed), then you are Abraham's offspring and (spiritual) heirs according to promise.

Galatians 6:1-2

KJV—Brethren, if a man be overtaken in a fault, ye which are spiritual, restore such an one in the spirit of meekness; considering thyself, lest thou also be tempted. Bear ye one another's burdens, and so fulfil the law of Christ.

AMPC—Brethren, if any person is overtaken in misconduct or sin of any sort, you who are spiritual—who are responsive to and controlled by the Spirit—should set him right and restore and reinstate him, without any sense of superiority and with all gentleness, keeping an attentive eye on yourself, lest you should be tempted also. Bear (endure, carry) one another's burdens and troublesome moral faults, and in this way fulfill and observe perfectly the law of

Christ, the Messiah, and complete what is lacking [in your obedience to it].

Galatians 6:10

KJV—As we have therefore opportunity, let us do good unto all men, especially unto them who are of the household of faith.

NIV—Therefore, as we have opportunity, let us do good to all people, especially to those who belong to the family of believers.

AMPC—So then, as occasion and opportunity open to us, let us do good (morally) to all people [not only being useful or profitable to them, but also doing what is for their spiritual good and advantage]. Be mindful to be a blessing, especially to those of the household of faith—those who belong to God's family with you, the believers.

Ephesians 4:1-3

NKJV—I, therefore, the prisoner of the Lord, beseech you to have a walk worthy of the calling with which you were called, with all lowliness and gentleness, with longsuffering, bearing with one another in love, endeavoring to keep the unity of the Spirit in the bond of peace.

NIV—As a prisoner for the Lord, then, I urge you to live a life worthy of the calling you have received. Be completely humble and gentle; be patient, bearing with one another in love. Make every effort to keep the unity of the Spirit through the bond of peace.

AMPC—I therefore, the prisoner for the Lord, appeal to and beg you to walk (lead a life) worthy of the [divine] calling to which you have been called—with behavior that is a credit to the summons to God's service, living as becomes you—with complete lowliness of mind (humility) and meekness (unselfishness, gentleness, mildness), with patience, bearing with one another and making allowances because you love one another. Be eager and strive earnestly to guard and keep the harmony and oneness of [produced by] the Spirit in the binding power of peace.

Ephesians 4:25

NKJV—Therefore, putting away lying, each one speak truth with his neighbor, for we are members of one another.

NIV—Therefore each of you must put off falsehood and speak truthfully to his neighbor, for we are all members of one body.

Ephesians 6:18

AMPC—Pray at all times—on every occasion, in every season—in the Spirit, with all [manner of] prayer and entreaty. To that end keep alert and watch with strong purpose and perseverance, interceding in behalf of all the saints (God's consecrated people).

Weymouth—Pray with unceasing prayer and entreaty at all times in the Spirit, and be always on the alert to seize opportunities for doing so, with unwearied persistence and entreaty on behalf of all the saints.

Brothers and Sister in the Lord

1 Peter 2:9

KJV—But ye are a chosen generation, a royal priesthood, an holy nation, a peculiar people; that ye should show forth the praises of him who hath called you out of darkness into his marvellous light.

AMPC—But you are a chosen race, a royal priesthood, a dedicated nation, [God's] own purchased, special people, that you may set forth the wonderful deeds and display the virtues and perfections of Him Who called you out of darkness into His marvelous light.

NASB—But you are a chosen race, a royal priesthood, a holy nation, a people for God's own possession, that you may proclaim the excellencies of Him who has called you out of darkness into His marvelous light.

1 Peter 3:8

KJV—Finally, be ye all of one mind, having compassion one of another, love as brethren, be pitiful, be courteous.

NIV—Finally, all of you, live in harmony with one another; be sympathetic, love as brothers, be compassionate and humble.

Weymouth—In conclusion, all of you should be harmonious, sympathetic, kind to the brethren, tender-hearted, lowly-minded.

1 John 1:7

KJV—But if we walk in the light, as he is in the light, we have fellowship one with another, and the blood of Jesus Christ his Son cleanseth us from all sin.

NKJV—But if we walk in the light as He is in the light, we have fellowship with one another, and the blood of Jesus Christ His Son cleanses us from all sin.

NIV—But if we walk in the light, as he is in the light, we have fellowship with one another, and the blood of Jesus, his Son, purifies us from all sin.

1 John 2:10

KJV—He that loveth his brother abideth in the light, and there is none occasion of stumbling in him.

NIV—Whoever loves his brother lives in the light, and there is nothing in him to make him stumble.

AMPC—Whoever loves his brother [believer] abides (lives) in the Light, and in It or in him there is no occasion for stumbling or cause for error or sin.

1 John 3:14

KJV—We know that we have passed from death unto life, because we love the brethren.

NIV—We know that we have passed from death to life, because we love our brothers.

1 John 4:7

NKJV—Beloved, let us love one another, for love is of God; and everyone who loves is born of God and knows God.

AMPC—Beloved, let us love one another; for love [springs] from God, and he who loves [his fellow

Brothers and Sister in the Lord

men] is begotten (born) of God and is coming (progressively) to know and understand God—to perceive and recognize and get a better and clearer knowledge of Him.

Weymouth—A new commandment I give you, to love one another; that as I have loved you, you also may love one another.

Family Scriptures
Quick Reference List

Blessings for Your Household - Chapter 1

The Gift of Marriage - Chapter 2

92

Family
Promises

Regarding Divorce

Husbands and Fathers - Chapter 3
Husbands

Fathering

Wives and Mothers - Chapter 4

Wives

Mothering

Conceiving Children

Parenting God's Way - Chapter 5

Promises for Children - Chapter 6

Family
Promises

Single—And Married to Him - Chapter 7

Brothers and Sisters in the Lord - Chapter 8

96

Family
Promises

Prayer for Salvation and Baptism in the Holy Spirit

Heavenly Father, I come to You in the Name of Jesus. Your Word says, "Whosoever shall call on the name of the Lord shall be saved" (Acts 2:21). I am calling on You. I pray and ask Jesus to come into my heart and be Lord over my life according to Romans 10:9-10: "If thou shalt confess with thy mouth the Lord Jesus, and shalt believe in thine heart that God hath raised him from the dead, thou shalt be saved. For with the heart man believeth unto righteousness; and with the mouth confession is made unto salvation." I do that now. I confess that Jesus is Lord, and I believe in my heart that God raised Him from the dead. I repent of sin. I renounce it. I renounce the devil and everything he stands for. Jesus is my Lord.

I am now reborn! I am a Christian—a child of Almighty God! I am saved! You also said in Your Word, "If ye then, being evil, know how to give good gifts unto your children: HOW MUCH MORE shall your heavenly Father give the Holy Spirit to them that ask him?" (Luke 11:13). I'm also asking You to fill me with the Holy Spirit. Holy Spirit, rise up within me as I praise God. I fully expect to speak with other tongues as You give me the utterance (Acts 2:4). In Jesus' Name. Amen!

Begin to praise God for filling you with the Holy Spirit. Speak those words and syllables you receive—not in your own language, but the language given to you by the Holy Spirit. You have to use your own voice. God will not force you to speak. Don't be concerned with how it sounds. It is a heavenly language!

Continue with the blessing God has given you and pray in the spirit every day.

You are a born-again, Spirit-filled believer. You'll never be the same!

Find a good church that boldly preaches God's Word and obeys it. Become part of a church family who will love and care for you as you love and care for them.

We need to be connected to each other. It increases our strength in God. It's God's plan for us.

Make it a habit to watch VICTORY Channel™ and become a doer of the Word, who is blessed in his doing (James 1:22-25).

About the Authors

Kenneth and Gloria Copeland are the best-selling authors of more than 60 books. They have also co-authored numerous books including *Family Promises,* the *LifeLine* series and *From Faith to Faith—A Daily Guide to Victory.* As founders of Kenneth Copeland Ministries in Fort Worth, Texas, Kenneth and Gloria have been circling the globe with the uncompromised Word of God since 1967, preaching and teaching a lifestyle of victory for every Christian.

Their daily and Sunday *Believer's Voice of Victory* television broadcasts now air on more than 500 stations around the world, and the *Believer's Voice of Victory* magazine is distributed to nearly 600,000 believers worldwide. Kenneth Copeland Ministries' international prison ministry reaches more than 20,000 new inmates every year and receives more than 20,000 pieces of correspondence each month. Their teaching materials can also be found on the World Wide Web. With offices and staff in the United States, Canada, England, Australia, South Africa and Ukraine, Kenneth and Gloria's teaching materials—books, magazines, audios and videos—have been translated into at least 26 languages to reach the world with the love of God.

Believer's Voice of VICTORY

When the Lord first spoke to Kenneth and Gloria Copeland about starting the *Believer's Voice of Victory* magazine...

He said: *This is your seed. Give it to everyone who ever responds to your ministry, and don't ever allow anyone to pay for a subscription!*

For more than 50 years, it has been the joy of Kenneth Copeland Ministries to bring the good news to believers. Readers enjoy teaching from ministers who write from lives of living contact with God, and testimonies from believers experiencing victory through God's Word in their everyday lives.

Today, the *BVOV* magazine is mailed monthly, bringing encouragement and blessing to believers around the world. Many even use it as a ministry tool, passing it on to others who desire to know Jesus and grow in their faith!

Request your FREE subscription to the *Believer's Voice of Victory* magazine today!

Go to **freevictory.com** to subscribe online, or call us at **1-800-600-7395** (U.S. only) or **+1-817-852-6000**.

We're Here for You!®

Your growth in God's WORD and victory in Jesus are at the very center of our hearts. In every way God has equipped us, we will help you deal with the issues facing you, so you can be the **victorious overcomer** He has planned for you to be.

The mission of Kenneth Copeland Ministries is about all of us growing and going together. Our prayer is that you will take full advantage of all The LORD has given us to share with you.

Wherever you are in the world, you can watch the *Believer's Voice of Victory* broadcast on television (check your local listings), kcm.org and digital streaming devices like Roku®. You can also watch the broadcast as well as programs from dozens of ministers you can trust on our 24/7 faith network—Victory Channel®. Visit govictory.com for show listings and all the ways to watch.

Our website, **kcm.org,** gives you access to every resource we've developed for your victory. And, you can find contact information for our international offices in Africa, Australia, Canada, Europe, Ukraine, Latin America and our headquarters in the United States.

Each office is staffed with devoted men and women, ready to serve and pray with you. You can contact the worldwide office nearest you for assistance, and you can call us for prayer at our U.S. number, +1-817-852-6000, every day of the week!

We encourage you to connect with us often and let us be part of your everyday walk of faith!

Jesus Is LORD!

Kenneth & Gloria Copeland

Kenneth and Gloria Copeland